LOST LANDS

KENNY ABDO

Fly!
An Imprint of Abdo Zoom
abdobooks.com

abdobooks.com

Published by Abdo Zoom, a division of ABDO, P.O. Box 398166, Minneapolis, Minnesota 55439. Copyright © 2020 by Abdo Consulting Group, Inc. International copyrights reserved in all countries. No part of this book may be reproduced in any form without written permission from the publisher. Fly!™ is a trademark and logo of Abdo Zoom.

Printed in the United States of America, North Mankato, Minnesota.
102019
012020

Photo Credits: Alamy, iStock, Shutterstock
Production Contributors: Kenny Abdo, Jennie Forsberg, Grace Hansen
Design Contributors: Dorothy Toth, Neil Klinepier, Pakou Moua

Library of Congress Control Number: 2019941602

Publisher's Cataloging-in-Publication Data

Names: Abdo, Kenny, author.
Title: Lost lands / by Kenny Abdo
Description: Minneapolis, Minnesota : Abdo Zoom, 2020 | Series: Guidebooks to the unexplained | Includes online resources and index.
Identifiers: ISBN 9781532129353 (lib. bdg.) | ISBN 9781644942888 (pbk.) | ISBN 9781098220334 (ebook) | ISBN 9781098220822 (Read-to-Me ebook)
Subjects: LCSH: Lost continents--Juvenile literature. | Cities and towns, Ruined, extinct, etc--Juvenile literature. | Mythical places--Juvenile literature. | Legends--Juvenile literature. | Ghost towns--Juvenile literature.
Classification: DDC 398.42--dc23

TABLE OF CONTENTS

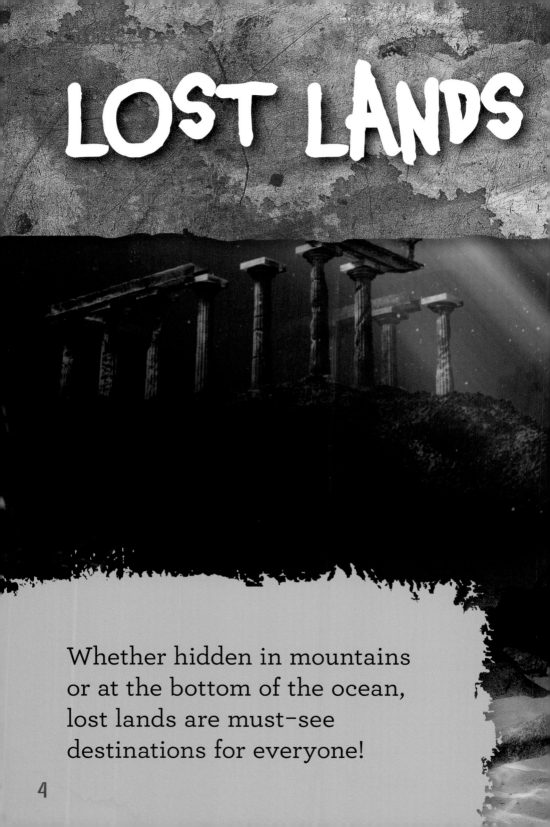

LOST LANDS

Whether hidden in mountains or at the bottom of the ocean, lost lands are must-see destinations for everyone!

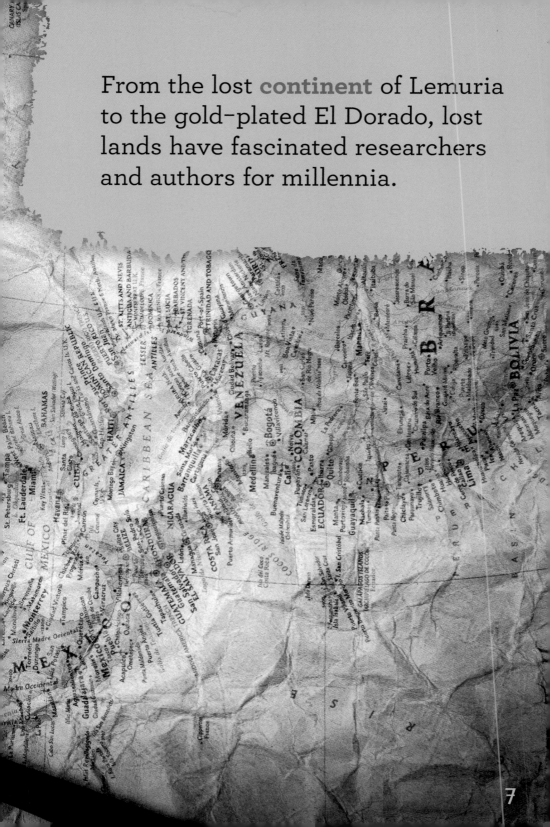

From the lost **continent** of Lemuria to the gold-plated El Dorado, lost lands have fascinated researchers and authors for millennia.

CLASSIFICATION

Lost lands can be classified in many ways. Some are considered otherworldly **planes** here on Earth. While the majority are mythical places pulled from **folklore** and religious texts.

Scientists have studied lost lands for centuries. Whether sunken **continents** or **civilizations** below Earth's crust, researchers believe there is more to learn about our history.

Many authors often use lost lands as **plot devices**. Others used them to prove our past. Ignatius Donnelly wrote *Atlantis: The Antediluvian World*. In it, he tries to prove that Atlantis is real and that we can all be traced back to it.

DECLASSIFIED

During the mid-1800s, scientists believed that there was a **continent** at the bottom of the Indian Ocean. It is known as Lemuria. A race of humans that had four arms and giant bodies roamed the land. They were thought to be the ancestors of modern humans and lemurs.

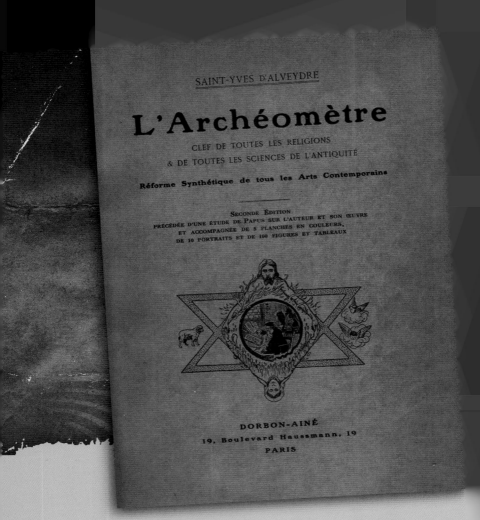

French occultist Alexandre Saint-Yves d'Alveydre believed Earth was hollow. Inside lies the land of Agartha. It is inhabited by many different races and **civilizations**. Agartha holds wealth and wisdom unlike anything we could ever imagine.

El Dorado was not always a place. It was a person. A man from Colombia covered himself in gold and sunk himself in a lake. Many explorers searched far and wide for "the golden one," or to discover the location of El Dorado.

Scholomance is a school of black magic. It is located in the mountains of Transylvania. Only ten students are admitted each year to the underground campus. And the dean is the Devil. This is one place you want to avoid summer school!

Deep in the **Scottish Highlands**, you will find the enchanting village of Brigadoon. It is known as a **utopia**. Brigadoon is visible for one day every one hundred years. Those lucky enough to come across it will never want to leave.

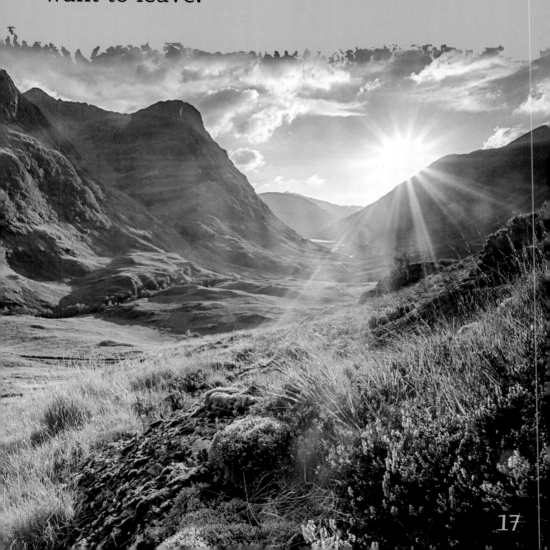

The most popular lost land is Atlantis. **Philosopher** Plato taught about it. He said the city had sunk due to its population's **hubris**. Atlantis has been studied for more than 2,000 years!

IN MEDIA

Lost lands have been the central setting for many major movies, TV shows, and books. You can also roam through them in several hit video games!

Lost lands have raised many questions scientists want to answer. And they have sparked the imaginations of authors for centuries. But don't pack your bags just yet. You'll never find them on a map!

GLOSSARY

civilization – a well-organized and advanced society.

continent – one of Earth's seven main land areas.

dean – a person at a school who is in charge of guiding students.

folklore – a story handed down from person to person.

hubris – to have an excessive amount of pride.

philosopher – someone who understands and teaches philosophy, which is an area of study that looks at logic, ethics, and reality.

plane – a level of thought, growth, and existence.

plot device – something in a story that moves the plot forward.

Scottish Highlands – the mountainous region of northwest Scotland.

Transylvania – a region of central Romania. It is most famous for its legend of Dracula.

utopia – an area that has the perfect qualities and conditions for its citizens.

ONLINE RESOURCES

Booklinks
NONFICTION NETWORK
FREE! ONLINE NONFICTION RESOURCES

To learn more about lost lands, please visit abdobooklinks.com or scan this QR code. These links are routinely monitored and updated to provide the most current information available.

INDEX